Riding
SCHOOL

Learn how to ride at a real
RIDING SCHOOL

LONDON, NEW YORK, MELBOURNE,
MUNICH AND DELHI

Designed and Photoshoot Directed by Lisa Lanzarini
Project Editor Catherine Saunders
Pony Club Consultant Nikki Herbert
Publishing Manager Cynthia O'Neill Collins
Category Publisher Alex Kirkham
Art Director Mark Richards
Production Jenny Jacoby and Kate Oliver

First published in Great Britain in 2003 by Dorling Kindersley Limited,
80 Strand, London WC2R 0RL
A Penguin Company

03 04 05 06 07 10 9 8 7 6 5 4 3 2 1

The publisher would like to thank the following for their kind
permission to reproduce their photographs:

(Key: l=left; t=top)

Superstock Ltd./Ron Dahlquist: 34tl.

All other images © Dorling Kindersley
For further information see: www.dkimages.com

A CIP catalogue record for this book is available from the British Library.

ISBN 0-7513-6965-9

Reproduced by Media Development and Printing, Ltd
Printed and bound at Tlaciarne BB, Slovakia

Discover more at
www.dk.com

Riding SCHOOL

Learn how to ride at a real
RIDING SCHOOL

Written by Catherine Saunders
Photography by David Handley

Contents

Introduction

If you already love horses or have always dreamed of learning how to ride, this book is for you! Riding is a fun and exciting activity for everyone to enjoy. Come and join the girls and boys at a real riding school and discover the wonderful world of horses.

Getting Ready

*O*livia loves horses! Today will be her first riding lesson and she is very excited. It's really important to be safe and comfortable when learning to ride so Olivia and her mum have been shopping for everything she needs. Olivia has put on her pretty blue shirt and new jodhpurs and can't wait to start her lesson.

Making friends

At the riding school, Olivia meets Holly and Alexandra, who will be learning to ride with her. Olivia starts to feel a bit nervous, as well as excited, but she is pleased that she has made some new friends.

A shirt with a collar will give Olivia's neck extra protection.

What to wear

The special trousers worn for riding are called jodhpurs. They have extra padding to protect the rider's knees. Long sleeved tops protect the rider's arms.

Warm, long-sleeved top

T-shirt with collar

Jodhpurs

Ankle length riding boots with smooth sole and heel

Riders do not have to wear body protectors, but Olivia, Holly and Alexandra want to be as safe as possible!

Hat

The hat protects the rider's head if they fall off. There are different hat styles and fashions all over the world.

Body protector

Gloves and stick

The Riding School

Before the lesson starts, the girls meet their teacher, Linda. She shows them all the different parts of the riding school and tells each girl which pony they will be riding. They can hardly wait! There is one more pupil for the beginners' class, but he hasn't arrived yet. Who will it be?

When the horses and ponies are not being used for lessons, they are "turned out" in the fields, where they can run about and graze freely.

The stables are clean and tidy. The horses can see what is going on around them but the stable doors are safely bolted.

The tack room

The saddle, bridle and other equipment used for riding are known as tack. The tack and tack room must be kept clean and tidy by the riders.

The indoor school

The outdoor school

The beginners' school

Paying attention

Linda takes the register
and tells the children how
to get to know the horses,
safely. However, someone
is not listening at all –
pay attention Dandelion,
you sleepy cat!

Who's Who

The class is almost ready to begin. Sammy, the final pupil, has arrived at last. He will be riding Bertie, who is very friendly. Olivia is delighted to be riding Honey, who is a very pretty pony. Holly thinks that her horse, Cullud, looks very funny with his brown and white patches. Linda tells Alexandra that her horse's name is Matilda but she prefers to be called Mattie!

Linda loves horses! She thinks that it is important to teach children to enjoy riding, as well as learning to care for the horses.

Older pupil

Sophie is 10 years old. She has been riding for three years and can trot, canter, gallop and even jump on her favourite pony, Danny. Later on she will show the beginners some of her skills.

Although Danny is a small pony, he is the perfect size for Sophie. She loves him because he is fast and very brave.

Little riders

Linda also has special lessons for children, such as Tom and Natalia, who are too young to control a pony on their own. She sits them on the gentlest ponies and guides them safely on a lead rein.

Mattie and Alexandra   Honey and Olivia   Cullud and Holly   Bertie and Sammy

13

Horses and Ponies

Horses and ponies are often measured in "hands" rather than centimetres. Ponies are smaller than horses – they are 14.2 hands or less. When learning to ride it is also a good idea to learn the special names for the parts of a horse, so that you know what the teacher is talking about!

Natalia is stroking Honey on a sensitive part of her nose, called the muzzle.

Linda holds Honey and Mattie together to show the class the difference in size between a pony and a horse.

1 *Tail*　　　**2** *Hock*　　**3** *Fetlock*　　　　　　　　　　　**4** *Frog*

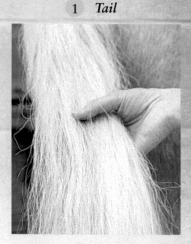

Just like your hair, ponies have their tails brushed and trimmed – sometimes they even have them plaited!

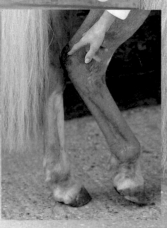

The hock bends to allow the hind (back) leg to move forward. At the same time, the fetlock bends the other way to lift the hoof off the ground.

This funny-looking part of the hoof helps ponies to grip.

9 Mane

10 Withers

The withers are a very sensitive part of a pony. Some ponies even like to be tickled here!

10

9

6

7

Looking at the ears can tell you a lot about a pony's mood. If the ears point forwards, like Honey's, the pony is happy and interested, if they point backwards, the pony is sleepy or bored. If a pony's ears are completely flat, that means she is very cross!

5 Hoof

6 Shoulder   **7 Elbow**   **8 Knee**

8

5

A pony's hooves are very strong, but for extra protection they are fitted with special metal shoes.

The shoulder and elbow are joints, like the hock, fetlock and knee. They are where two or more bones meet and help the pony to move.

The knee bends to allow the pony to lift the foot and move it forwards and backwards. This is very important when jumping.

Colours and Markings

Comet is a chestnut horse, which is a special shade of brown. He has a lovely golden mane and tail. What a handsome horse!

Horses and ponies can be a variety of beautiful colours, all with special names. They may also have some interesting markings, usually on their face or legs. Learning some of the special terms will help the class tell the difference between their favourite horses and ponies.

Archie

Twigs

Sega

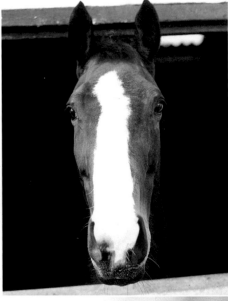

Stripe
Twigs has a long, thin white mark, known as a stripe.

Blaze
Sega has a thick white stripe, called a blaze.

Star and snip
Archie is very proud of his handsome face! The white mark on his forehead is called a star. He also has a cute mark on the tip of his muzzle, called a snip.

Some ponies have white marks on their legs, called socks. If these marks continue above the knee, they are called stockings.

Socks

Ermine mark

These spots above the hoof are known as ermine marks.

Honey is palomino.

Danny is dun.

Cullud is skewbald.

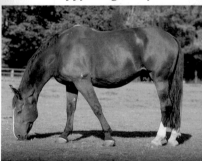

Dappy is light bay.

Bertie is grey.

Pablo is dark bay.

Colourful coats

There are lots of different shades, each with special names, but bay is the most common colour for a horse or pony. Strangely enough white horses are known as greys!

17

Getting the Pony Ready

Although the children are ready for the lesson, their ponies are not! Linda tells them that ponies should be groomed every day to keep their coat, skin and hooves healthy. After some gentle grooming, the ponies are ready for their saddles and bridles to be put on – this is called tacking up.

Grooming kit

Saddle

Tacking up

It is very important that the saddle and bridle are put on correctly. The pony must be comfortable and the rider should be safe. The bit should not hurt the pony's mouth and the saddle should not slip.

First Olivia places the saddle over Honey's withers and slides it into position.

Next Olivia fastens the girth under Honey's belly, making sure that is not too tight.

Linda has shown Olivia how to put the bridle on. The bit goes in first and then Olivia pulls the bridle carefully over Honey's ears.

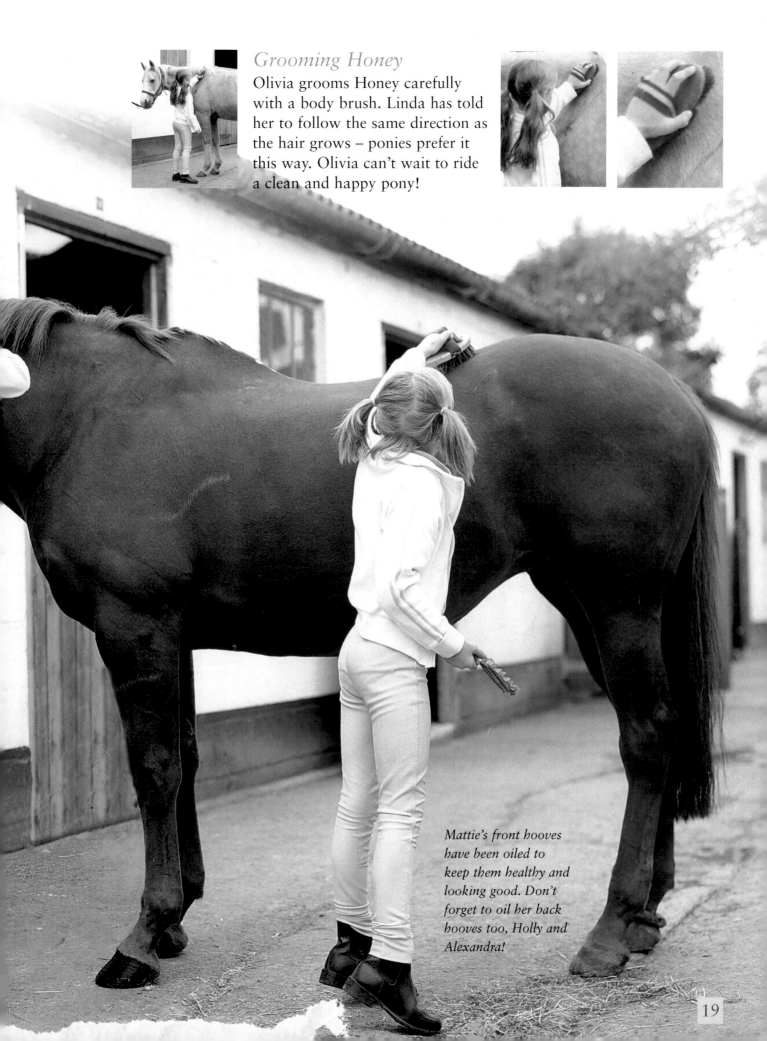

Grooming Honey

Olivia grooms Honey carefully with a body brush. Linda has told her to follow the same direction as the hair grows – ponies prefer it this way. Olivia can't wait to ride a clean and happy pony!

Mattie's front hooves have been oiled to keep them healthy and looking good. Don't forget to oil her back hooves too, Holly and Alexandra!

19

The Basic Positions

It is finally time for Olivia to start riding! The first thing that she must learn is how to get on and off Honey safely. This is called mounting and dismounting. It is also very important that Olivia and Honey feel good together so Linda shows Olivia how to sit correctly in the saddle, how to hold the reins and where to put her feet in the stirrups.

Olivia and Honey are ready to begin their first lesson together. Olivia has put on her protective hat and vest and can't wait to start!

Mounting and dismounting

Olivia is a little nervous but Linda shows her exactly what to do. She has checked that Honey's girth is tight, so the saddle will not slip, and adjusted the stirrups. Olivia is ready.

How to mount and sit

1 Hold both reins in your left hand and stand on the left side of the pony. Bring the stirrup towards you, with your right hand.

2 Put your left foot into the stirrup. Next, turn your body to face the pony's side and grasp the saddle with your right hand. Push off the ground with your right foot, so that you are standing in the stirrup.

3 Swing your right leg over the pony's back. At the same time, turn your body to face forwards and lower yourself into the saddle. Remembering to keep hold of the reins, feel for the other stirrup with your right foot. You can use your right hand to help, if you need it.

Make sure that the reins are not twisted, and hold them with your thumbs on top.

Keep your heels down in the stirrups.

Olivia is doing really well, she is concentrating hard but having fun, too!

How to dismount

4 When you have mounted, it is important to sit properly. Hold the reins in both hands and sit up straight, in the middle of the saddle. Keep your head up and your elbows in and most importantly of all – relax!

1 To dismount, take both feet out of the stirrups and hold the reins in your left hand.

2 Lean forward and swing your right leg over the pony's back. Bend your knees and land with both feet together.

3 Well done, you have dismounted safely! Give your pony a pat to say thank you.

Sammy gives Bertie a gentle pat.
They are becoming great friends!

Warming Up

To *help the children* and ponies get to know each other, the teacher shows them some fun warm up exercises. Olivia, Holly, Alexandra and Sammy must learn to understand their ponies so they can control them gently, calmly and safely. A good rider can tell their pony what to do by using their voice, hands and legs. These instructions are known as "the aids".

Lining up

After they have all mounted safely, Linda tells the class to line up. When all the riders are sitting in the correct position, with the reins held properly, they can begin the warm up exercises. Pay attention Honey and Bertie, this is no time for slouching!

Stretching exercises

To make Olivia and Sammy feel more relaxed, Linda shows them some fun stretching exercises. It helps them to trust Honey and Bertie and feel more confident on horseback.

Touch your toes

Go on Olivia, you can do it!

Touch the tail

Stretch Sammy – almost there!

22

Right leg over first.

Other leg now, Olivia!

All the way round, let's go again!

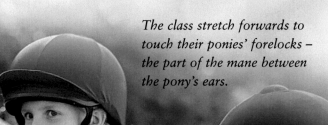

The class stretch forwards to touch their ponies' forelocks – the part of the mane between the pony's ears.

Around the world

The riders take both feet out of the stirrups and hold the front of the saddle with their right hand and the back of the saddle with their left hand. Then they swing their right leg over the front of the saddle and turn all the way round!

School markers
Markers like this are positioned around the school to help the children ride together, safely. The teacher uses the different letters to direct the riders.

The Riding Lesson

After the warm up, the class practise walking around the school. Group lessons like this help the children become aware of other riders and horses. They must remember everything that Linda has told them: Come on everyone, sit up straight, keep your heels down, hold the reins securely and most importantly of all – relax and smile!

Alexandra and Mattie

Holly and Cullud

1 Not too close.

2 Safely passed.

1 In a straight line

Passing side by side

Holly and Alexandra show how riders should pass each other without bumping their horses! Notice how the riders pass on the left and keep a safe distance between the horses. This is called riding left hand to left hand.

Changing the rein

Alexandra is riding in front, so she is known as the leader and Mattie is the lead horse. Linda ask the class to change direction so Alexandra uses her legs and reins to steer Mattie. The rest of the class follow. This is called changing the rein.

2 Alexandra leads

3 All turning

Olivia and Honey

Sammy and Bertie

The class are ready to go but they must remember to listen to Linda at all times!

25

Faster and Faster!

When a child first learns to ride, they begin by sitting on the horse or pony in walk. Later on, when the rider is more confident, they will learn to trot, which is faster than walking. More advanced riders then learn to canter, which is even faster, and finally to gallop, which is faster still!

Alexandra is a very brave rider and she is ready to learn how to trot, with Mattie's help!

Trotting

There are two different ways to trot – sitting and rising. First Alexandra learns the rising trot, which is easier as the rider lifts up slightly in the saddle, in time with the pony's strides. Later she must learn the sitting trot because it helps with other skills, such as cantering.

To go from walking to trotting, Alexandra sits up straight, shortens the reins and squeezes firmly with her legs.

The trot has two beats to one stride because ponies have four legs. Ponies move their legs in diagonal pairs, so when one front hoof and opposite back hoof are on the ground, the other diagonal pair are off the ground.

Cantering

Linda shows the class how to canter, using Sega. She begins in a steady sitting trot. To show Sega that she wants him to canter, Linda sits tall and brushes her outside (left) leg slightly behind his girth, and at the same time nudges him with her inside (right) leg, near his girth. Unlike trotting, cantering has three beats per stride.

1 The outside (left) hind leg pushes the horse forward to canter.

2 The outside (left) foreleg and the inside (right) hind leg are on the ground. The inside (right) foreleg is leading.

Experienced riders can enter competitions. This rider is smartly dressed because she is about to enter a dressage competition, which tests the rider's control of the horse.

This horse has his mane and tail plaited, so that he looks neat and pretty for a dressage competition.

"I love riding faster and faster!" Sophie

Sophie loves cantering and can't wait to learn how to gallop!

Galloping

When a rider has perfected cantering, they can learn to gallop. Unlike the other gaits, the rider bends forward, lifting their weight out of the saddle.

3 All the weight is now on the the inside (right) foreleg.

4 Finally there is a moment of suspension when all the feet are off the ground. Then the sequence starts again.

Learning to Love Horses

Riding and caring for horses can bring pleasure to many different people. It is good exercise and great fun for for people of all ages, from young people like Olivia and her class, to adults and people with special needs. Linda and her team ensure that riders of all abilities are safe and well looked after at the riding school.

Olivia's little brother, Tom, wants to learn to ride, just like his big sister.

Tom and Natalia

Tom and his best friend, Natalia have come to the riding school to meet the horses. But Linda has a wonderful surprise in store for them – they are going to have a special lesson of their own!

Special classes

Horse riding is great fun for everyone! Some children have special needs and riding is a great way for them to exercise and develop new skills. It is a lovely sunny day and Kate is really enjoying herself riding Comet!

Olivia introduces Tom to some of the horses and ponies at her riding school. He dreams of riding a big horse like this one, called Kerry.

Kate needs extra help to mount Comet. Two helpers make sure that she feels safe and relaxed, at all times.

"I love riding just like Olivia!"
Tom

Tom and Natalia are having a great time!
They are riding, just like Olivia and her friends, but Linda has Danny and Honey on the lead rein so she is actually in control of the ponies.

“_Horses and ponies love to
canter about and play when
they are turned out in the
fields. It is a beautiful sight!_**”**
Linda

Sophie Learns to Jump

A rider must be really comfortable on horseback before he or she is ready to start jumping. The most important things when learning to jump are confidence, balance and trust between rider and pony. Sophie is very excited when Linda tells her that she is finally ready to start jumping!

Two standard jumps

Trotting poles

First Sophie learns to jump over trotting poles, which are laid on the ground. They help her get used to the rhythm of jumping and develop her balance.

A jumping saddle

The first jump

Sophie is ready for her first proper jump. Ponies are naturally able to jump so all Sophie needs to do is canter towards the low jump and lean forward into the correct jumping position, as Danny takes off. When they have completed the jump, Sophie pats Danny to say, "thank you".

Sophie leans forward, with a straight back, her head up and her weight in the stirrups.

Refusal

Don't worry if your pony refuses to jump – it happens to everyone. You will probably fall off your pony at some point too, just like all the greatest riders!

Danny refuses to jump.

❝ *I trust Danny and he loves jumping!* ❞
Sophie

Cross country

These rustic fences are called cross country fences. Experienced riders often enter competitions where they jump over a variety of fences, including hedges, walls, gates and sometimes even in and out of water!

33

Western Riding

Olivia and her friends have been learning "European" style riding, which is what most children learn, at least to begin with. Western riding is a different way of riding and it is popular all over the world. It started with cowboys in the USA and Central America, who have to drive cattle over long distances.

Western rider

This Western rider is wearing traditional Western trousers, known as chaps and a hat called a Stetson. Western riders do not have to wear hard protective helmets, like Olivia and her class, but it is always safer to wear a helmet, especially when you are first learning.

Western equipment

There are a few main differences between European and Western riding and equipment. The saddle has a high front and back, and the bridle has a curved bit, or no bit at all. The reins are also different and are usually held more loosely.

Western saddle

Western bridle

A Western rider's legs hang straighter down the horse's sides than in European riding, to make the rider more comfortable during long rides.

In Western riding the reins are usually held in one hand and used as little as possible. However, a young horse, like this one, needs two hands to control him.

This is Patrick and his horse, Archie. They are learning to ride Western style, at Linda's riding school. Olivia and the class are very interested and have come to watch the lesson.

Western style

The class can see that Western riding is very different from the European-style, which they are learning. The leg "aids" are used in a different way and the reins are used gently on the neck to ask the horse to move sideways, change direction quickly or stop.

Alexandra is excited when Patrick lets her ride Archie. She would love to learn Western-style riding but knows that she must perfect European-style first!

Out and About

Olivia is very lucky because her riding school is in the middle of some beautiful countryside. After a few lessons, Linda thinks that the class is confident enough to ride out. This is known as a hack. The class are really excited, but they must be even more careful when they are outside the safety of the riding school.

Olivia can't wait to ride Honey in the countryside, it will really test everything that she has learnt so far!

Hacking out

When riding out Linda and the class stick to proper footpaths, known as bridleways. The children stay close behind Linda, so that she can warn them about low branches or tree roots that might trip the ponies. The class must not get too close though – they don't want the ponies to bump into each other!

Linda leads the class because they should never ride out without an experienced adult.

Alexandra always shuts the gate as there may be animals in the field.

Opening and closing gates

Alexandra shows how to open and close a gate, without dismounting. First she positions Mattie alongside the gate and holds both reins in one hand. Then she bends down to open the gate. She moves Mattie around, using her legs, and passes through the gate. Mattie is now next to the other side of the gate and Alexandra simply changes hands and bends down to close the gate.

Road safety

Riders need to be especially safety-conscious outside the school. If riding on the road, they should wear fluorescent vests, like these riders, so that they are clearly visible to cars and other road-users, at all times.

"*Going on a hack is great fun. Honey loves riding in the woods.*"
Olivia

After the hack, Olivia turns Honey out in the fields, with Danny and Bertie.

Untacking the Ponies

Although the riding lesson has finished, the class still have some work to do. They have to untack the ponies and cool them down before they can be turned out into the field. Looking after the ponies is hard work, but very important!

Untacking is the opposite of tacking up. It means to remove the saddle and bridle. Olivia has untacked Honey and is carrying the heavy saddle very carefully.

Cleaning tack

Holly carefully cleans Cullud's bridle. It is not as much fun as riding, but she knows that caring for horses is an equally important skill to learn.

Cleaning Honey

Olivia cleans Honey's eyes, nose and mouth with a special sponge. She must make sure that she washes the eyes and rinses the sponge carefully.

Like most ponies, Honey has a very sensitive muzzle and loves to be stroked there. Olivia thinks that it is very soft and smooth.

Here Olivia uses the scraper to remove the sweat from Honey's coat.

When all the lessons have finished for the day, the horses are turned out in the fields, where they can run about freely.

39

Feeding Time!

The children are very excited because they are allowed to feed the ponies for the first time! In the wild ponies usually eat grass, but at the riding school they have to do lots of extra work so they need lots of energy-packed food. They are fed two or three times a day.

This bucket is very heavy so Alexandra and Holly must be careful not to spill any of the food.

Types of food

Each pony at the riding school has a special diet suited to his or her personal needs. Ponies are fed a variety of different foods to keep them fit and healthy. Some ponies are fed pre-mixed foods from special feed merchants.

Dried grass is called hay. Ponies need extra hay in winter, when it is too cold for them to graze outside.

Honey deserves a little treat! The hay is hung up in a net so that Honey cannot tread on it.

Here are some of the types of food ponies like to eat but they would not eat them all at one time!

A little treat

Ponies also love fruit and vegetables. Holding his hand flat, Sammy gives Bertie a carrot. This is a safe way to feed a pony.

pony nuts

coarse mix

barley (must be cooked)

sugar beet (must be soaked)

chaff

(chopped hay and straw to add bulk to the food)

Caring for the Horses

Horses and ponies need lots of special care to keep them healthy and happy. They need the right food, plenty of exercise and lots of love! But like people, ponies are individuals and sometimes they need extra attention.

These rugs keep the ponies warm after a hard day of lessons.

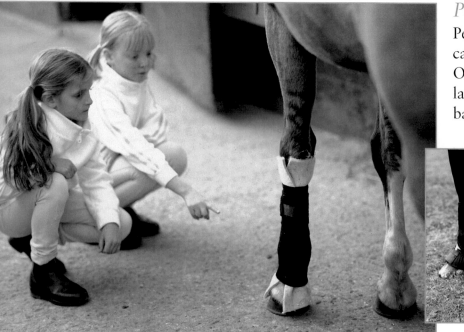

Poor Pepsi!
Pepsi has a sore foreleg and she can't walk properly. Holly tells Olivia that this is known as being lame and now that Pepsi's leg is bandaged, she will be better soon.

Special boots
This horse is wearing brushing boots and over reach boots. Brushing boots protect the pony's legs from knocking against each other. Over reach boots protect the front hooves from being trodden on when jumping or galloping.

Hamlet is allergic to flies. This mask protects his eyes but it has small holes so he can still see through it.

Apollo is even more allergic than Hamlet and needs this special coat to protect his whole body and stop him from itching.

Lungeing

Lungeing, using a rope, is a way of exercising young horses who have never been ridden before. It is also used for horses who are recovering from injury.

Swimming

Swimming is also a good way of keeping horses fit. It can strengthen their muscles after injury or illness and is great fun for them, too!

New shoes

Horses and ponies wear metal shoes to protect their hooves. A blacksmith or farrier, like Adam, fits them with new shoes about every six weeks.

1 Removing the old shoe

2 Filing the hoof

3 Preparing the new shoe

4 Fitting the shoe

5 All fixed!

Having a new shoe fitted does not hurt the horse, but Adam must be careful to avoid the frog and the sensitive inner hoof.

Fun and Games

Sometimes, even young riders take part in special competitions, called gymkhanas. They are very exciting and the winners receive pretty rosettes. Today Linda decides that the class has worked really hard and sets up some games for them. It is another test of the skills that they have learnt during their lessons.

Everyone is a winner
The children are looking forward to the mini-gymkhana. They don't know yet but Linda has rosettes for everyone.

Olivia reaches for the dish.

This is a close race – it looks like Alexandra and Mattie are catching up!

Peg and run!
The object of this game is to ride up to the dish on the pole, attach the peg and then race back to the finish line. It is a test of the rider's control over the pony and the pony's speed.

That's right Olivia! Great work Honey!

Olivia and Honey are heading for the finish line. Come on Alexandra and Mattie, see if you can catch them!

Alexandra is in the lead.

But Olivia is catching up fast.

Olivia wins the game!

Flag the bucket

This game is really simple. Each of the riders has a flag which they must drop into the bucket and then race back to the finish line. If they miss the bucket, they must go back to the start and get a new flag.

> "Playing games with my friends is fun and we are getting better all the time!"
> Olivia

45

Glossary

A

Aids – the voice, leg and hand signals that a rider uses to control the horse.

B

Bit – the mouthpiece attached to the bridle.
Blacksmith – also known as the farrier, this person fits horses with special metal shoes.
Bridle – a head harness worn by a horse.

C

Canter – a three-beat gait that is faster than a walk or trot but slower than a gallop.
Chaps – leather trousers that cover the legs only, worn by cowboys and western-style riders.
Cross country – a competition over a variety of natural hedges, fences, walls, gates and rails for the horse and rider to jump over.

D

Dismounting – getting off the horse.
Dressage – a competition which tests the correct training of the rider and horse.

G

Gait – a type of movement.
Gallop – a four-beat gait and the fastest of all.
Girth – the strap that holds the saddle securely, underneath the horse. It has two buckles on each side for extra safety.
Gymkhana – mounted games competition for young riders.

J

Jodhpurs – special trousers for riding which have extra padding inside the knee.

H

Hack – riding out in the countryside.
Hands – a special measurement used for horses and ponies. (1 hand = 10.2 cm/4 in)

L

Lame – when a horse has hurt its foot or leg.
Lead rein – this is attached to the bit so the pony can be led by a teacher.

M

Mounting – getting on the horse.

R

Reins – leather straps, fastened to the bit and held by the rider.

S

Saddle – a special seat which makes it more comfortable for the rider to sit on a horse.
Stetson – a hat worn by cowboys and Western riders.
Stirrups – metal loops which are attached to the saddle to support the rider's feet.

T

Tack – a term for the saddle, bridle and other riding equipment.
Trot – a diagonal two-beat gait.
Turned out – this is when the horses run around freely in the fields.

W

Western riding – a style of riding made popular by cowboys in the USA.

Index

Acknowledgements

*Dorling Kindersley would like to
thank the following for their help
in the preparation and production
of this book:*

Toby and Jennifer Greenbury, owners of
Checkendon Equestrian Centre, Lovegrove's
Lane, Checkendon, Reading RG8 0NE
(www.checkendon.f9.co.uk) for their kind
permission to photograph the book there.

Special thanks to centre manager Linda Tarrant for her
invaluable guidance and wonderful hospitality during
the photoshoot; Pony Club consultant Nikki Herbert
for her expertise and enthusiasm; the riding stars
Alexandra, Holly, Natalia, Olivia, Sammy, Sophie and
Tom; photographer David Handley and his assistant
Anthony; Mary Atkinson for copy-editing assistance.

An extra-special thanks to Honey, Mattie, Bertie,
Cullud, Danny, Archie and all the other wonderful
horses who posed so patiently for us.